Edinburgh); *365* (National Theatre Of Scotland/Edinburgh International Festival); *Yarn* (Grid Iron/Dundee Rep); *Helter Skelter* (Tramway/Music at the Brewhouse); *Green Whale* (Licketyspit); *Arabian Nights* (Young Vic); *The Cosmonaut's Last Message to the Woman He Once Loved in the Former Soviet Union* (Paines Plough); *Sleeping Around, Crazy Gary's Mobile Disco, Crave* (Paines Plough); *Caravan* (National Theatre of Norway); *Afore Night Come* (Theatr Clwyd); *The Importance of Being Ernest* (Nottingham Playhouse); Twelfth Night (Central School of Speech and Drama); *Othello* (Watermills Theatre); *King and Marshall* (Bloomsbury Theatre); *Four Saints in Three Acts* (Trinity Opera). Costume design for theatre includes: *The Weavers* (Gate Theatre). Georgia has also done set design for photography and worked as a lecturer in the History of Art and Design.

Gordon McIntyre (Songwriter/Musician) Gordon is a member of the band ballboy with whom he has released five albums and also has a solo side project named Money Can't Buy Music (album forthcoming). He has toured extensively across the UK, Europe and the USA and his music has been used in films and television shows in the UK, Australia and in the USA. He has recorded numerous radio sessions with the band and solo including five Peel Sessions as well as sessions for BBC Scotland, xfm and other stations around the UK. Gordon also works as a Primary School teacher in Edinburgh. For more information visit www.ballboymusic.com.

Matthew Pidgeon (Bob)
Matthew trained at RSAMD. For the Traverse: *Kyoto* (co-produced with Oran Mor), *The Nest*. Other theatre includes *The Wonderful World of Dissocia, Realism* (National Theatre of Scotland); *The Man Who Had All the Luck, The Wizard of Oz, Pinocchio, The Glass Menagerie* (Royal Lyceum Theatre, Edinburgh); *The Lying Kind* (The Royal Court); *The Tempest* (Tron Theatre); *Edward Gant's Amazing Feats of Loneliness* (Drum Theatre Plymouth); *8000m* (Suspect Culture); *Born Guilty* (7:84). Film credits include *The Winslow Boy, State and Main, A Shot at Glory, Chopsticks*. Television credits include *Fiona's Story, Holby City, Taggart, Casualty, This Morning with Richard not Judy*. Radio credits include *Kyoto, The Black Sheep, The Lion of Chechnya, Devastated Areas, McLevy, Kaffir Lilies, The Holly and the Ivy, Greenmantle* (all BBC).

For their help on
Midsummer
(*a play with songs*)
the Company would like to thank

Katherine Mendelsohn, Renny Robertson, Gabriel Bartlett,
Jo Timmins, Caroline Newall, John Tiffany, NTS Workshop
all of whom helped to develop the show on its journey
to the stage.

SPONSORSHIP AND DEVELOPMENT

We would like to thank the following
corporate funders for their support

To find out how you can benefit from being
a Traverse Corporate Funder, please contact
Fiona Sturgeon Shea, Head of Communications,
on 0131 228 3223 / fiona.sturgeonshea@traverse.co.uk

The Traverse Theatre's work
would not be possible without the support of

The Traverse Theatre receives financial assistance from:

The Atlantic Philanthropies, The Barcapel Foundation,
The Misses Barrie Charitable Trust, The Binks Trust, The Craignish Trust,
The Cross Trust, The Cruden Foundation, James Thom Howat
Charitable Trust, The John Thaw Foundation, The Lloyds TSB Foundation
for Scotland, The Peggy Ramsay Foundation, Tay Charitable Trust,
The Thistle Trust, The Weatherall Foundation

For their continued generous support of Traverse
productions, the Traverse thanks:

Habitat
Marks and Spencer, Princes Street
Camerabase

ARE YOU DEVOTED?

**Our Devotees are: Joan Aitken, Stewart Binnie,
Katie Bradford, Adrienne Sinclair Chalmers,
Adam Fowler, Joscelyn Fox, Anne Gallacher,
Keith Guy, John Knight OBE, Iain Millar,
Gillian Moulton, Helen Pitkethly, Michael Ridings,
Bridget Stevens, Walton & Parkinson**

The Traverse could not function without the generous support
of our patrons. In March 2006 the Traverse Devotees
was launched to offer a whole host of exclusive benefits
to our loyal supporters.

Become a Traverse Devotee for
£29 per month or £350 per annum
and receive:

- A night at the theatre including six tickets, drinks and a
  backstage tour

- Your name inscribed on a brick in our wall

- Sponsorship of one of our brand new Traverse 2 seats

- Invitations to Devotees' events

- Your name featured on this page in Traverse Theatre Company
  scripts and a copy mailed to you

- Free hire of the Traverse Bar Café (subject to availability)

Bricks in our wall and seats in Traverse 2
are also available separately. Inscribed with a message
of your choice, these make ideal and unusual gifts.

To join the Devotees or to discuss giving us your support
in another way, please contact Fiona Sturgeon Shea,
Head of Communications, on 0131 228 3223 /
fiona.sturgeonshea@traverse.co.uk

Charity No. SC002368

TRAVERSE THEATRE – THE COMPANY

David Greig

and

Gordon McIntyre

Midsummer

(a play with songs)

faber and faber

First published in 2009
by Faber and Faber Limited
74–77 Great Russell Street, London WC1B 3DA

Typeset by Country Setting, Kingsdown, Kent CT14 8ES
Printed in England by CPI Bookmarque, Croyon

A CIP record for this book
is available from the British Library

ISBN 978–0–571–25361–6

2 4 6 8 10 9 7 5 3 1

MIDSUMMER

(a play with songs)

Four days will quickly steep themselves in night;
Four nights will quickly dream away the time.

Shakespeare
A Midsummer Night's Dream

Narrative dialogue is in plain type.

Italics indicate real-time dialogue.

Songs are indented in italics.

Word songs – that is to say, stories that have
a musical backing – are indented in plain type.

A slash indicates that dialogue overlaps
or is spoken simultaneously.

(*Stage directions are italicised in parentheses.*)

ONE

LOVE WILL BREAK YOUR HEART

Love will break your heart
Love will break your heart in two
Love will break your heart
It doesn't matter what you do

Love will break your heart
Love will break your heart in two
Love will break your heart
But sometimes you want it to

TWO

It's Midsummer

In Edinburgh.

It's raining

And there's these two people having sex –

Bob and Helena.

They've only just met.

They met a couple of hours ago in a pub.

You could call it a pub it was more of a wine bar –

One of those cellar bars,

A brasserie.

Where lawyers go.

Helena's waiting for a man – she's sitting at a corner table – dressed in an understated but nevertheless elegant black dress – poking at an untouched avocado salad – nursing a glass of forty-pound New Zealand Sauvignon blanc – watching the rain fall –

Thinking about the secret that she can't even tell to herself –

Watching the rain fall and fall and fall like it's never going to stop

Which it won't by the way –

Not once,

Not once for the whole weekend.

9.17.

(*Beep*.) Helena receives a text – she looks into the mirrored surface of the wine cooler for about twenty seconds and then she turns her face to the crowd in the bar and makes eye contact with –

Bob.
Bob's out on a piece of business which we can't really talk about because it's strictly speaking illegal.

It's actually illegal.

Bob's waiting to pick up the keys to a stolen car. Bob hates waiting, hates this place, hates all these lawyery types poking about with salads and forty-pound bottles of wine and generally lawyering themselves around the room –

Helena's a lawyer – specialising in divorce.

Bob's divorced – somewhat bitterly – we'll come to all that later. Just for now here's Bob – alone at the bar – black beer in front of him – black thoughts inside him –

reading a damp paperback copy of *Notes from the Underground* by Dostoevsky – to cheer himself up.

Helena looks at Bob,

Body all tied up in knots – radiating hostility

And she thinks – 'Perfect.'

So she walks over to him and she says:

Excuse me, would you like to come back to my place and have extremely wild, uninhibited sex with me?

—

She does not say that.

Effectively she says that.

Let's meet Bob –

Robert Victor Morris Liddell Hope Macartney

Otherwise known as

Medium Bob

On account of him having no apparent defining features

Unlike say Nose Jackson or Moleneck Stevie Lamont.

Medium Bob works on the fringes of Edinburgh's criminal underworld mostly doing odd jobs that involve fabricating stories.

He's a piss artist –

A storyteller –

A liar.

At school Bob was a star. He had a talent for poetry that was spotted by the editor of the school magazine.

Bob was the editor of the school magazine.

He wore black eyeshadow and grandad shirts. He back-combed his hair and formed a band called The Bloody Chamber. In 1987 they had a demo tape played on Radio Four.

Radio Forth.

Same difference.

In 1987 Bob was going out with Freda Bastianelli, the most beautiful girl in the school.

In 1987 Bob bought a guitar and an InterRail ticket and a Greek fisherman's cap and set off to busk his way around Europe.

In 1987 Bob was the brightest star in the glorious firmament that was Broughton High School.

1987 was Bob's year.

It's all been downhill since then.

Bring Bob your promise – it shall be dimmed. Bring Bob your hope – and it shall be lost. Bring Bob your right and surely it shall be made wrong – if you want something spoiled, soiled, hurt, broken or maybe just made more ugly – ask Bob.

Which is why

On the Friday of this Midsummer weekend

At 9.17

Bob is not about to read extracts from his travel writing to an appreciative audience in Waterstone's

But is sitting here in Whighams Wine Cellars,

Body all tied up in knots, radiating hostility,

Waiting for Old Mister Pettit to turn up and give him the details of whatever strictly speaking illegal act he's

supposed to undertake this weekend for his boss – Big
Tiny Tam Callaghan –

Watching the rain fall

Fall and fall like it's never going to stop,

Which is when Helena comes over to him – all perfume
and control – and says:

Hi.

Sorry?

Hi.

Hi.

Is this seat taken?

No.

Do you mind if I –

If you –?

Sit –

Right – OK – sit – no.

No?

I don't mind – on you go.

I've got a bottle of wine here –

Right.

I need someone to help me drink it.

Oh.

Dostoevsky?

Yes. Do you like him?

No.

What's your name?

Me? Robert – Rob – Bob – fuck.

Bob Fuck?

Bob.

Bob, can I be honest with you?

Of course –

I'm at a loose end tonight and you look like you might be at a loose end too. How would you like to come back to my place and have extremely wild uninhibited sex with me?

—

She so does not say that.

That is so effectively what she says.

Three hours earlier, Helena's flat –

Helena looks at herself in the mirror for the first time in something like six weeks and thinks to herself – OK – she thinks – if I was him and I saw her – that woman – me – I would think – 'yes' – only just – but 'yes' – I'll go home with her tonight – that woman – me.

That's what Helena thinks.

(Beep.) See you 8.30. Wear something red. Smiley face with a wink.

Eight o'clock, Helena's driving. On the radio a story about some fireman visiting a child in hospital, sick with leukaemia.

Shit.

8.01.

Helena's crying. Recently Helena has noticed herself crying – suddenly, briefly and without warning – which is strange because Helena is not a sentimental woman.

Normally Helena has no time for weeping, no time for wailing. She's seen in her job the way women weaken themselves with sentiment – she's seen how love erodes the ground on which a woman stands until one day the earth beneath her is suddenly washed away and whoosh! the family lawyers – whoosh! – the children bundled into taxis – whoosh! – the tears. Helena's seen them all – the dazed, confused women – cattle she calls them – mooing their way across the fields of marital disaster – lowing helplessly in the fog – lost. No – Helena is not a sentimental woman,

These recent crying jags notwithstanding.

Helena is nobody's cow.

9.17.

Helena catches sight of her reflection in the silver of the wine cooler – she takes a long hard look at herself – such a long hard look she gives herself she could turn herself to stone – Medusa – before she finally comes to the conclusion that – yes – despite everything – if I were him I would still say 'yes' to her – that woman – me.

—

(*Beep.*) *Have to cancel. Trouble at home. Can't get away. Sad face.*

—

OK. OK – so –

—

(*Text.*) *No worries. Totally understand. These things happen.*

—

FUCK.

—

(*Text.*) *Sad face.*

Helena really really didn't want to be alone tonight.
Please. Not tonight.

Send.

Because if Helena's on her own then she might have to
confront the secret she can't even tell to herself.

Hi.

Sorry?

Hi.

Hi.

Is this seat taken?

No.

Do you mind if I –

If you –?

Sit –

Right – OK – sit – no.

No?

I don't mind – on you go.

I've got some wine here –

Right.

Can't drink it all on my own.

No.

Would you like some wine?

Thank you.

What?

Nothing –

Dostoevsky?

Yes. Do you like him?

No.

What's your name?

Me? Robert – Rob – Bob – fuck.

Bob Fuck?

Bob.

Would you like to get drunk with me tonight, Bob?

—

That's what she said.

That's what she said, but what she meant was:

Would you like to get really drunk with me tonight, Bob?
Really really drunk. So drunk so that we forget who we
are and where we are and then – just when we're on the
point of oblivion – let's fuck – let's have wild uninhibited
sex – and because we're drunk it won't matter whether
it's any good or not because neither of us are going to
remember it anyway and besides you're so not my type
so after tonight there's no chance of us seeing each other
ever again.

Hmm?

Bob.

What do you say?

Yes, I say yes.

THREE

THE SONG OF OBLIVION

Tonight the devil on my shoulder's gonna
Reach right over
Slip a noose around the angel and just
Push him overboard

Out into emptiness
Watch his feet swing into space
And lower down his grinning face
And say and say

Where are your wings now?
Where are your wings now –?

And so I tell my devil what I need
Give me this night and I'll agree
That in the morning bright and cold
I'll offer up my damaged soul

And follow him where darkness leads
It's what I need, it's what I need
It's what I need, it's what I need
It's what – I – need

Just give me drink
Give me darkness
Give me pain
Then take it all away
Give me darkness
Give me pain
And take it all away

Drink and darkness
Give me pain
Take it all away

Drink and darkness   *The devil always knows the way*
Give me pain   *I should have thought of this*
Take it all away   *before*

Drink and darkness   *The devil always knows the way*
Give me pain   *I should have thought of this*
Take it all away   *before*

FOUR

11.56.

Helena's left her car in the Castle Terrace car park and together they've staggered back to Marchmont through the rain too drunk to notice the waterfalls under their feet, they've stumbled and giggled and slurred and staggered up the steps of the close and in the door and they don't know how exactly it happened – but the next thing they know they're in bed –

And you know when sex goes really really well? – You know when you forget who you are and everything just melts into a warm tangle of unfamiliar skin and a sort of endless unfolding of now? You know when sex is just a great big beautiful now?

That's what it was like –

Until –

  (*They hear.*)

Elmo wants a cuddle. Elmo wants a cuddle.

What?

Nothing.

  (*A strange voice.*)

Elmo wants a cuddle.

Shhh.

  (*And again.*)

Elmo wants a cuddle.

  (*And then Bob finds its source.*)

Elmo?

Sorry.

Elmo!

Ignore it.

You've got Elmo in your bed?

He belongs to Brendan, my nephew.

Right.

Sorry.

No, it's OK, it's funny.

He must have left him here when he was over this afternoon.

Right.

DON'T THROW HIM!

What?

Sorry – it's just – let's just put him here.

OK.

Now where were we?

Wait –

What?

Can you turn him to face away? Sorry.

OK.

Thanks.

I just feel funny with him looking at me.

Right.

Now where were we?

—

Piss cock tits.

Is something wrong?

Wrong? No? God, no. This is – great.

Great.

Great.

Great.

Great.

Concentrate, Helena.

Come on, Bob, do your job. Get back in the zone.

Focus – *fuck me.*

OK.

Oh God you're good.

Oh God – she thinks I'm good.

Oh yeah.

Come on – I am good –

Mmmmm.

I'm an animal – a wolf – a ravening wolf –

He's trying so hard.

Marauding across a primeval plain –

The least you can do is moan, Helena –

Hunting – capturing my woman –

Ooaahh!

I claim her.

That was a shit moan, Helena, do it again –

Claim her?

Ooooaaaaahhhhhyessss!

What am I, Fred Flintstone?

This is hopeless. / This is hopeless.

Bring out the old standbys – Kim Wilde –

—

Clare Grogan –

—

Kim Wilde and Clare Grogan –

—

Kim Wilde and Clare Grogan in a hot girl-on-girl orgy –

—

Except Kim Wilde's not a girl any more. She's a fully grown woman –

—

And she's the gardening correspondent for the *Observer*.

Bob?

Maybe I should become a gardener.

Just go somewhere far away and garden.

Bob?

Hmm.

Oh.
Mmmm.

Come on, Bob. / Come on, Helena.

Oh. / *Oh.*

Oh. / *Oh.*

Yes. / *Yes.*

Yes. / *Yes.*

Yes. / *Yes.*

Yes. / *Yes.*

Yes. / *Yes.*

Yes. / *Yes.*

YES! / *YES!*

Thank God. / Thank God.

FIVE

Afterwards Helena's lain in Bob's arms in the dark and
felt the loneliness steal back over her – that feeling of
being gripped, winded almost, that she sometimes gets –
and she's remembered Brendan sitting on the bed beside
her that afternoon – the way he kept touching his knee
and then his forehead – the way he kept talking, asking
about astronauts – telling her how he'd love to be an
astronaut and how she said: 'In a spaceship, Brendan?'
And he said: 'No, Auntie Helena, I want to be an
astronaut outside the spaceship on an air-supply tube,
I want to be floating, Auntie Helena, I want to float and
look inside the windows.' Knee forehead – knee forehead –
and she asked him: 'Who's inside the spaceship, Brendan?'
And he said: 'You are. Auntie Helena, you're inside.'

What?

Nothing.

Are you crying?

It's the drink. It's just the drink.

Hey hey hey.

It's just the drink.

And – whatever it was that made her cry, whether it was the drink or something else – some other secret she wasn't giving up to him – Bob's found that holding a crying woman and saying –

—

It's OK. It's OK.

—

– has made him feel surprisingly – because normally he'd want to run, of course – surprisingly – sprint actually – surprisingly – get the fuck out of there, Bob! She's a weeping nutter, run! That's normally what Bob would think – but tonight, holding this particular woman and feeling the particular unfamiliar warmth of her against him drifting into sleep, Bob has found that he feels surprisingly OK.

—

Shh.

It's OK. It's OK. It's OK.

Bob?

Yeah.

You'd better go. Eh?

Yeah.

Sorry.

SIX

THE SONG OF BOB'S COCK
(spoken word over music)

And so I'm walking home in the middle of the
night and I'm – you know – I'm disorientated –
I'm confused – and the first glimpses of the
morning are just coming up over the meadows –
and I need a piss so I go up to a tree except it
won't come – it can't come because – well –
it's maybe morning glory or maybe just the
memory of the night but there it is anyway –
standing up straight and just looking at me –
which is not necessarily that unusual except
that, you know – it actually is looking at me.

And I realise that I'm staring my cock straight
in the face.

And so I'm looking at it and then – it/he starts
to talk to me – It starts to talk to me –

'Look at yourself, Bob – look at the way
you've lived your life, man – your doing all these
things and they're not fulfilling – they're not –
worthwhile – you're a fucking underachiever,
Bob.'

And then it gets on to my love life and it says:

'And what about the women, Bob? All these
women that you never commit to – I mean, is
that what you really want, Bob – is that what
you really want?'

And I'm trying to answer and I'm saying to my
cock: 'It's not all about what I want, really.
I mean – you only get one life, right? I mean,

I'm supposed to be having adventures – I'm supposed to be having experiences, right?'

I'm trying to explain – because I just want to piss – but I can't – not while he's up on his high horse like this – I'm trying to explain that what I was doing, it was for him! And I'm expecting him to come around to my way of thinking – I'm expecting him to say:

'You know I never thought of it that way – now I see it your way, Bob – thanks very much – thanks for all the good times.'

But he doesn't say that, he says this instead:

'Bob. You and I are not young men any more – I mean we have a combined age of seventy, and I'm fed up. I'm a bit fed up of all the different hands that have touched me and the different lips that have kissed me. I'm fed up of being in different women – I'm fed up of being in different beds, in different places – I'm fed up of all of that. All I want is a pair of hands I can get used to, a pair of hands that I am familiar with – a pair of hands that will, you know, guide me through the years. That's what I want, Bob – you know – our adventuring days – maybe they're over. And maybe that's okay.

'And I have to admit – that I never thought of it like that before.'

SEVEN

Saturday, 10.00 a.m.

Midsummer morning on Marchmont Road and we find Helena in her fourth-floor flat vomiting into the bowl of her expensive lavatory and with every retch she's piecing together what happened the night before.

Oh God.

What she said when he –

Oh God.

And what she did when –

Oh God.

And how much she –

Oh God.

And with every retch the anaesthetic tide of drink ebbs from her brain and finally leaves behind it, washed up and naked on the shores of her consciousness, the secret she can no longer hide even from herself –

Oh God – oh God – oh God.

Sitting there on the sink top – an unopened packet of Clearblue Strip.

Oh God.

Ignore it, children – not nice – don't look – turn your eyes away and let's just keep walking down the beach.

HANGOVER SONG

If my hangover was a country it would
*   be Belgium*
If my hangover was a town it'd be Harthill

> *If my hangover was a smell it would be –*
>   *one that never leaves*
> *And if my hangover was a boy it would*
>   *be you*
>
> *If my hangover was a god he'd be vindictive*
> *If my hangover was a dog it would be dead*
> *If my hangover was a film it would be –*
>   *four hours long and French*
> *And if my hangover was a boy it would be you*
>
> *Ba bada bum*
> *Ba bada bum – etc.*

It's Midsummer morning and across town in a basement flat just off Leith Walk Bob's desperately trying to work out which combination of painkillers and health foods can make this awful nausea go away when Bob too is also forced to face a secret.

'Dear Mr Macartney – Our records tell us that you are thirty-five years old today. We are offering all our patients on their thirty-fifth birthday the chance to attend our practice nurse for a "Well-Man MOT".'

Today is Bob's birthday.

OK – it's not so much a secret as just the fact that no one knows it's Bob's birthday because no one knows Bob well enough to care.

So Bob's just contemplating the fact that his arrival into middle age will take the form of a cold latex-covered finger up his arse, when there's a knock on his door.

Tam.

Bob.

Big Tiny Tam Callaghan punches Bob in the face with a thick fist tightly covered in a brown calf-skin driving glove.

That's for leaving old Mr Pettit sat waiting on his own in Whighams all night. When are you going to get some fucking responsibility, Bob? Jesus.

Big Tiny Tam Callaghan was a small man, but still took up his fair share of space in the world. Tam has a son, Tam Jr., Tiny Tiny Tam, who, perhaps through good nutrition, has grown up to be a bigger man than his father, and so an Oedipal paranoia has recently crept into Big Tiny Tam's heart.

(*Tam kicks Bob.*)

Big Tiny Tam Callaghan just feels he ought to be asserting more authority over his organisation.

Get up. I've got a fucking job for you.

I've got a car for you to sell.

It's pink.

Don't fuck it up.

> *If my hangover was an angel it would be*
> > *fallen*
> *If my hangover was a ship then it would sink*
> *If my hangover was a feeling it would be –*
> > *last-minute defeat*
> *And if my hangover was a girl it would be you*
>
> *Ba bada bum*
> *Ba bada bum – etc.*

Helena's also got a job to do.

Shit.

Helena's sister's getting married today at twelve.

I'm late.

Helena's a bridesmaid.

Oh God. I'm late.

Shouldn't be too difficult – she just needs to turn up on time – smile and keep a civil tongue in her head.

Fuck shit piss cock tits.

This'll be Helena's third sister to get married. Plus the three times her brother's been married as well. Making a total of eight times bridesmaid.

Swallow the rage, Helena.

Always the bridesmaid –

Smile

It should be easy – all she has to do is drive to the cathedral – cluck and coo – say 'Don't we all scrub up nicely?' – affect to be moved by the ceremony – stand for photographs – ask after people's children – refer mooningly to 'little ones' – adopt a demeanour of lightness and modest gaiety. And when they say – and they will say – 'You'll be next, Helena?' and 'She met him on the internet you know, Helena,' and 'Why don't you go on the internet, Helena?' Helena must smile and nod.

Total dissociation – mind out of body –

Above all Helena must resist the temptation to say:

Fuck it, internet dating. Total desperation. I give them a year.

That's her job.

Swallow the rage.

10.55.

Fuck! Fuck! Fuck! Fuck! Fuck!

Helena's just realised she left her car in the Castle Terrace car park.

> *Ba bada bum*
> *Ba bada bum – etc.*

EIGHT

Sighthill Industrial Estate.

Bob's standing next to a stolen pink convertible in the rain – trying to sell it to a man from Glasgow.

– Take a look, take your time, feel free –

It's pink.

Pink, yes.

Why do you have a pink car?

Apples – pink ladies – I'm in the apple trade. I sell apples, deliver them, in fact, to people in offices. Pink ladies, pink, it's a very eye-catching colour, isn't it?

Why are you selling . . . ?

Bottom's fallen out of the apple market – really – bees, all the bees dying, bees pollinate the apple trees, no bees no trees –

That's a shame –

Isn't it? When I was a kid the summers were full of bees – exactly – you used to get bees on your pieces, you used to get bees in the grass, didn't you? You used to stand on the big bees in the grass – you did. Come to think of it, it's years since I stood on a bee –

How much?

Fifteen grand in cash like we said on the phone –

Done.

Fifteen thousand pounds in a Tesco bag.

Problem?

A Tesco bag, not even a bag-for-life, a bog-standard slightly ripped thin polybag?

No, no problem.

Thirty-eight minutes till the bank shuts.

Fuck.

Run! / Run!

A lot of people seem to take up running in their mid-thirties. Men and women in sports clothes weave in and out of the pedestrians, they bounce on the spot at traffic lights, their iPods clicking. And we ask ourselves – why do they run?

A few years ago maybe you were late for something important, you don't remember what but there were no buses and no taxis and so instead of walking he broke into a run.

You call it a run, it was more a kind of limited half-jog, but as inhibition fell away it became a full-blooded sprint down George Street, then – somewhere besides Grays the Ironmonger your body forced itself into some kind of lift off and your feet flew above the pavement in a moment of pure childish joy.

Before – smack – your anaerobic oxygen ran out and he hit the wall. Breathless, he stumbled, staggered towards St Andrew's Square in the rain, humiliated, and he thought –

Whoever remembers being breathless in their childhood? Whoever remembers walking?

Childhood – if it's about anything surely it's about a plenitude of breath?

Is that gone now?

Is this what I am now?

Is this what being adult is?

Breathless always, gasping, slow?

And so, when you see them – the runners – weaving and glistening through the crowds, you might think, 'Look at them, the fools, they're trying to run away from death' – but they're not – they're honestly not – they're running towards something –

And sometimes – when the road and the rhythm and pace is just right – they lose the boundaries of themselves and catch it just for a moment –

Childhood.

So you imagine Helena running.

Helena's trying to make it from Marchmont to St Mary's Cathedral in just under twenty minutes. On Helena's website profile she says she 'works hard and plays hard'. But 'play', in that context, doesn't mean squash or anything like that. 'Play' in that context means drinking and smoking.

So you imagine Helena running – holding her shoes – her stockinged feet mud-spattered in the puddles – sprinting through The Meadows – furious.

Now you imagine Bob running – he'd be fit, wouldn't he? Bob's a criminal – you'd think, but no – that's a common misconception about criminals – in truth criminals are rarely fit, they're just young. So you imagine Bob running red-faced and wheezing – barrelling down George Street.

Oh my fucking God.

And then for both of them the rain, of course, the rain which is always such an awful washer away of a person's illusions.

At 11.55 a.m. on Midsummer Saturday as the cathedral bell begins to toll –

The bank alarm begins to buzz –

11. 56.

The ushers take their seats –

11.57.

The manager stands at the door with the key –

11.58

The bride takes her father's arm –

And the bank doors are locked.

11.59.

Rain and running

Breath and body

Desperation and loss

Twelve noon

It's too late.

FUCK! / FUCK!

Too late. Too late. Too late.

NINE

So here's the question: you've got fifteen grand of Big
Tiny Tam Callaghan's money in a ripped Tesco's bag and
the bank's not open till Monday morning – what would
you do?

You'd bang on the door of the bank like a mad tramp.

You'd show the manager the money, you'd half open the
bag and point to the bundles of cash and you'd mouth:

I have to make a deposit.

What?

I have to make a –

Wait a minute –

And as the manager walked away you might think – great – she's gone to reset the alarm and let me in or something.

Security!

And that's when you might see, lumbering towards you on the other side of the glass, a security guard.

Bob? Is that you?

Shit shit shit shit shit.

Eyebrows Thompson.

Medium Bob!

Eyebrows!

How you doing?

Oh fine, you?

Fine, yeah.

Weather!

Lot of money in that bag.

Yeah.

Better keep that safe.

Right.

See you later, Medium Bob.

See you later.

Damn.

How the fuck did Eyebrows Thompson ever get a job in a bank?

Consider the facts:

1 – Eyebrows Thompson has seen the money.
2 – Eyebrows Thompson is best mates with Knee Campbell.
3 – Knee Campbell is a completely fearless psychopath.
4 – Knee Campbell knows where you live.

What would you do?

Hold that thought.

12.05.

Cathedral steps.

Auntie Helena?

Brendan.

You were late, Auntie Helena.

I know, Brendan.

You're sweating, Auntie Helena.

Thanks.

Your sweat smells of beer.

Brendan!

Mum won't let me stay in church in case I scream. I've to stand at the back. Do you like my new camera?

It's lovely.

Auntie Selina gave it me.

Please don't point it at me any more, Brendan.

Auntie Selina said I'm official photographer today.

Did she? No – Brendan, please. I said –

Have you been sick, Auntie Helena?

No.

Is that sick?

It's not mine.

Auntie Selina said you were probably drunk last night as usual.

Did she?

See how there's so much of everything, Auntie Helena? See how there's so much of everything and it's all everywhere? Well, if you put it inside a camera it goes inside a square – that's what a camera does, Auntie Helena – it puts everything inside a square. Without a square how do you know where to start and where to stop? See?

Brendan, please don't point the camera at the sick.

12.15.

Faced with a conundrum, some people find answers in instinct or experience, other people turn to God – but when Bob faces a conundrum Bob thinks: 'What would I do if I was faced with this conundrum and I was the main character in a Hollywood film?'

OK – here's the premise:

Bob can't tell Big Tiny Tam the money's not safe, because Tam will go mad at him for fucking up again, and Tam's Oedipally sensitive at the moment, so he's likely to get violent. Bob doesn't want to go home, because Knee Campbell might come and get him.

Bob needs – sanctuary . . .

Certificate 18. Starring Bob as Bob. Where do you go when there's nowhere left to hide?

I gotta find a cathedral. Now!

Exterior – cathedral steps – day.

You / You –

Sorry / Sorry –

I was just / I was just –

It's OK / It's OK –

What are you . . .? / What are you . . .?

Long story / Long story –

You look / You look –

Wet / Wet –

Hungover? / Hungover? –

Yeah. / Yeah.

Wedding? / Wedding.

Sister?

Sister.

Nice. / Nice.

Look, last night – / Last night –

Yeah / Yeah –

Mad / Mad –

Yeah –

Drunk / Drunk –

Big mistake.

Big mistake.

I'm already – I have a – I'm with someone.

Right –

Good.

Yeah.

Good.

Good.

You're not? / Are you . . .?

Me? / Me . . .?

No, / No,

Totally OK –

Totally / Totally –

Totally.

Well, I'd better go –

Yeah –

See you around –

Yeah –

Actually –

What?

No.

What?

Actually, no, look, I'm hungry, are you hungry, they do a good breakfast at the Conan Doyle. Why don't you join me?

There was an experiment done once where a group of students were wired up to computers and asked to either waggle or not waggle their little finger in response to a given signal.

What the researchers found was that the finger-operating area of the students' brains didn't show activity until a millisecond or so after the finger had begun to move.

They didn't decide and then move.

They moved and then decided.

You think you're making a decision but, in fact, whatever happened – it was already something you were going to do.

All you're doing is justifying yourself after the fact.

So when Bob looks at Helena and he says:

Actually, no, look, I'm hungry, are you hungry, they do a good breakfast at the Conan Doyle. Why don't you join me?

Bob is rationalising that to be a decision he's taking because he wants to seek sanctuary inside Helena's expensive flat –

But it turns out Bob didn't make any decisions!

When Bob saw Helena in her bridesmaid's dress on the cathedral steps all wet and forlorn-looking, it turns out he was always always going to say:

Actually, no, look, I'm hungry, are you hungry, they do a good breakfast at the Conan Doyle. Why don't you join me?

He had no choice.

And when Helena looked at him, clutching his Tesco bag like a mad tramp, and she said –

No. Best not, eh?

That was always how it was going to turn out.

Well, enjoy the happy occasion.

What? Oh, that – fuck it – internet dating – total desperation – I give it a year.

Life deals us the cards and it turns out we don't even play them, we simply turn them over and see what we've got.

The pack gets shuffled when you're born and all the rest's just a slow unwinding. You might think life's a game of poker but in fact it's game of patience.

Let's turn over the next card.

Auntie Helena – what does 'I'll give it a year' mean?

Brendan!

When you were speaking to the man you said, 'I'll give it a year.'

No, I didn't.

Yes, you did. You said, 'I'll give it a year.'

Brendan, please, shhhh.

No, you said. 'I'll give it a year.'

Brendan, shut up.

NOOOOOOOO!

Brendan.

Next card –

Brendan slips.

Next card –

Brendan falls.

Next card –

Brendan's covered in sick.

Next card –

Brendan screams.

Ahhhhhhhhhhhhhhhhhhh!

It turns out Brendan has a hygiene thing, a germ thing.

Brendan, it's OK. You're all right.

Get off! Don't hurt me again! Get off!

Next card –

The cathedral doors open, bride and groom and extended family emerge into the light to see Brendan taking his clothes off and screaming and touching his knee and his forehead and very loudly repeating the course of events in an attempt to put them back inside his mental square and so make sense of them –

Auntie Helena hit me and threw me in her sick.

Auntie Helena hit me and threw me in her sick.

'Oh, that – it's an internet thing – I give it a year,' that's what she said.

'Oh, that – it's an internet thing – I give it a year,' that's what she said.

If this were a scene in a Hollywood film, the camera would now draw away, upwards, to frame a wider shot and we would see on the cathedral steps a cluster of golden bridesmaids gathering around a naked screaming twelve-year-old boy.

We would see the bride's face crumple, we would see the groom and ushers scatter in confusion and in the middle of it all we'd see Helena – a still point in a world of chaos –

But it isn't a scene from a film – and so in fact the scene is just horrible – awful – the worst thing you could imagine happening to you – just a mess of shame and disgrace.

If this were a scene in a Hollywood film there would be confetti.

At least we can have confetti.

(*Confetti.*)

Love will break your heart
Love will break your heart in two
Love will break your heart
It doesn't matter what you do

Love will break your heart
Love will break your heart in two
Love will break your heart
But sometimes you want it to

Cut to:

Interior – The Conan Doyle Bar – Day.

Yes, Tam, I did the job, Tam. Yes, money in the bank, Tam, yes, no problem, Tam.

Bob looks at a plate of half-eaten breakfast.

Yes, Tam. Thanks, Tam.

Bob pokes a fork at a fried egg.

Yes, it is my birthday, how did you know that, Tam? Thirty-five, Tam, Yes, Tam, I do look older. Yes, Tam, it's the hair, Tam, all downhill from here. Well, cheery-bye, Tam, see you Monday, Tam, as usual.

As usual.

Interior – Bob's Head – Day.

The light from the egg that hits Bob's eye and travels through a soup of vitreous humour to Bob's retina sending a sparked bundle of electricity down the optic nerve and into his brain.

'Egg.'

The egg message speeds through endless corridors of grey matter past the flashes and sparks of synapses connecting in the dark –

Finally a door –

On the door, the words 'Department of Philosophical Underpinnings.'

Good morning, ladies and gentlemen, and welcome to the annual conference of Bob's. This year's topic: to celebrate Bob being thirty-five.

'Is this it?'

Let's welcome to the podium, please – Bob!

Thank you, Bob.

—

Consider the egg. Consider the chicken. Egg becomes the chicken – chicken becomes egg – and so on – endlessly – life is metamorphosis – life is change.

—

Now consider Bob.

—

Bob too was once an egg, now he is a fully grown man: two states of being so utterly different from one another that you might think they prove that Bob too is in a constant state of change. Proof, if you like, that 'this' is not 'it'. And yet – and yet – and yet –

—

Let's look at Bob aged three –
Five –
Ten –
Fourteen –
Let's look at Bob now.

—

Every cell in Bob's infant body has died and been replaced and yet Bob is still unquestionably Bob. Paranoid.

Defeated. Breathless. Alone. Bob's 'Bobness' was already contained within the egg. It seems there are many ways of being but there is simply no escape from being Bob. This, it would seem, is, in fact, it.

—

Any questions – Bob?

Bob. I've noticed a lot of middle-aged guys take up running when they hit thirty-five. Do you think it's possible Bob could take up running?

Thanks, Bob.

No – Bob will talk about taking up running, he'll buy the shoes even, but he'll never actually do it. That's Bob, I'm afraid.

—

Bob?

What about Bob's book of poetry?

Yeah, right. Ha ha ha. Sorry I'm just – no – the book of poetry thing – look, it'll never happen. Next question – Bob?

Bob – what are the implications of this being it?

Basically we face a long slow haul towards death. Every day will hold fewer surprises than the last. Our body will decay irreversibly. We will become less open to new ideas. We will become increasingly aware of decay and waste – some of you may already have noticed the extent to which you can actually smell shit everywhere now? In the street. In the house. On your breath. Disappointment will become our default position as each bright dream of our youth is snuffed out one after the other after the other.

That's a bracing analysis, Bob. What can we do to at least mitigate some of the effects you describe?

We can drink, Bob. Essentially, I advise us to keep drinking.

Should we take drugs? Bob?

Sadly I think we're too old for drugs. The danger of a cocaine-induced heart attack is simply too great. No, I think drinking is the best available long-term option.

See you Monday, Tam, as usual.

> *Love will break your heart*
> *Love will break your heart in two*
> *Love will break your heart*
> *It doesn't matter what you do*
>
> *Love will break your heart*
> *Love will break your heart in two*
> *Love will break your heart*
> *Sometimes you want it to*

Wait! New information – something new coming in: on the left – doorway of the pub –

12.59.

Helena.

Bob.

—

OK, so – I know I knocked you back and I realise I'm covered in sick but I'm on the run from a wedding party and I need to lie low for a while and so – I wondered if the offer of breakfast still stood.

BANG!

Ignore that – that's just the one o'clock gun.

TEN

Here's Bob and Helena walking through Princes Street Gardens holding an umbrella between them.

You'd think they were lovers – walking through parks – huddling under umbrellas.

But Bob and Helena are not lovers.

Of course they're not lovers and they're never going to be lovers.

Bob knows this because he knows no woman as beautiful as Helena would ever make the mistake of sleeping with Bob twice.

And Helena knows this because Helena watches romantic comedies. In a romantic comedy there has to be conflict between the protagonists.

He was an Alaskan oil man

And she was a Greenpeace activist.

Get the hell out of my way, lady, I've got a well to drill.

Damn you and your filthy oil.

Without oil, lady, there's no heat. And up here in Alaska, it gets pretty cold at night.

It's the way the couple have to resist their feelings that Helena finds sexy. It's something about the holding back,

Wanting but not wanting to want.

That just does it for her.

So anyway, Helena knows that she and Bob can't possibly be sexually compatible. Because they agree.

For three hours they can't stop agreeing.

They agree that that breakfast was really nice and surprisingly good value at 4.99.

They agree that this rain is mad.

They agree they should buy an umbrella.

They agree that it would be nicer to walk along Princes Street Gardens.

They agree that it's funny the way – once you've slept with someone – there's like no – sexual tension? So – you can just hang out and relax and things don't have to be – so – yeah . . .

They agree that they should sit inside the shelter and look at the castle.

They agree that the shelter smells of piss.

They agree that neither of them fancies the other.

Although they agree that they're both actually quite fit looking and that it's totally weird that they don't fancy each other but anyway they don't, so . . .

They agree that marriage is a hopeless waste of time.

And that love is actually just another word for 'need' and that when people say 'I love you' they say it because they want the other person to say it back to them to make them feel good and it's actually quite an aggressive thing to say.

They agree that it's amazing, this being Bob's birthday, because it was Helena's birthday only last month.

They agree that it's amazing that they're both thirty-five!

They agree that thirty-five's a shit age because it's, you know, is this it? Is this the shitty hand of cards I've been dealt – don't you think?

They agree that at thirty-five you have to accept that you're not going to be any of the things that haven't already become –

Like they agree that at thirty-five you really know you're never going to be an Olympic gymnast like Nadia Comaneci.

They agree that at thirty-five you know you're never going to read your poetry to an audience of girl students in Waterstone's.

They agree that at thirty-five you're not going to suddenly start baking cakes for babies' birthdays, you're obviously going to keep buying them from the Co-op on the corner despite what your sister says because actually it's not as if the kids give a fuck.

And they agree that at thirty-five you know that you're never going to buy a guitar and get on to the ferry to Belgium and spend a year just busking around Europe, you know, just playing some songs – you could probably make twenty quid a day and if you had a tent – that would be enough.

They agree that they both first kissed a member of the opposite sex in Princes Street Gardens – and that – oh my God, it's totally amazing because it was actually on the same bench.

They agree that it was this bench.

(*Silence.*)

They agree that, you know, you really like someone when you're comfortable being silent with them.

They agree that, Jesus! they've been talking for ages and that really now, they'd better, well – you know – get on.

They agree that Bob should chum Helena to her car.

They agree that 'chum' is an Edinburgh word.

When they finally get to Helena's car in the Castle Terrace car park and the ticket machine says the cost is twenty-four pounds they agree that that's completely scandalous.

And when the machine's screen says in bold type:

CHANGE IS POSSIBLE

They agree that it's funny to have a parking machine doling out philosophical advice.

Change is possible.

And when the machine's not taking cards and Bob offers to pay they agree Helena will pay him back sometime.

And then they both agree that she won't pay him back because they won't see each other again and that that was just one of those things you say to be polite like 'See you around' and they both agree that that's a shame because – well, because.

And when Bob reaches into the Tesco bag and peels a couple of twenties off of a bundle of notes and Helena can't help it, she sees the money, and she says:

What exactly is it you do, Bob? No – don't tell me – it's maybe better I don't know.

Bob agrees.

See you around.

Stay.

What?

Stay – don't go home –

Bob, that's –

Help me spend the money.

This money. In this bag. I've never had fifteen grand in a bag before. Imagine what we could do with fifteen grand in a bag and a night on the town.

Let's spend it.

All of it.

In a night.

Bob –

I live in a rented flat – I run strictly speaking illegal errands for a boss who's a wanker – I'm thirty-five. Helena, if I don't do something now I never will – and all the things I've never done will stay undone and then one day I'll take a breath and after it I'll realise there isn't another one coming – and at that moment, I'll remember the day I had fifteen grand in a bag.

Help me spend the money, Helena.

I'll buy a guitar and a ferry ticket to Belgium and we'll spend it and then on Monday morning I'll be gone. We'll never see each other again.

—

So what do you say?

Yes, I say yes.

ELEVEN

So this is the legendary lost weekend – this is the story you tell your grandchildren – the story that gets passed down through the generations and gets bigger and better with every telling. 'Tell me about the letters of love, Auntie Helena.'

'No, tell the part about the dancing lobsters – no, Bob, here, Bob, bondage! Do the bit about Japanese rope bondage –'

And the more you tell the story the more it becomes a story. All the rough edges get worn away and the details mixed up to make them better –

Bob says that truth isn't so important in a story. Bob thinks what matters is the feeling. When he tells the story he tries to capture the feeling. Bob likes to tweak the details.

But Helena really does want to remember. Helena loved that night and she feels the memory of it slipping away and that makes her sad and so every time she tells it she tries to remember it. She fights for every detail.

Starting with the drink.

Champagne, Chablis, some sort of port, fifty-year-old Macallan –

It was too early for clubs or restaurants so we went to Oddbins in the West End and I said, 'What's the best wine in the shop, what are the absolute peaches?' And so I showed him the money – you should have seen his face – and he totally gets into it – he's up and down the ladder getting bottles down. These bottles are like a hundred pounds each and the assistant's totally 'Try this one – and this one' – and, you know, we've bought as many as we can carry, and when we're leaving the shop he's smiling and he says, 'Enjoy the drinking,' and –

He looked so sad when we left. He had a sort of lopsided smile. He really cared about wine. I just thought it was a shame he couldn't drink it with us.

So Helena persuades him to close the shop and the three of us go back to the shelters in Princes Street Gardens and we start popping the champagne and knocking back the port and offering it in plastic cups to the goth kids who're hanging out there, and the assistant's going:

Do you get the overtones of rosemary coming through on the nose there and all the tannins?

And the goth girls are going:

Have you got any blackcurrant to go with that?

Somehow we started moving up towards the High Street. Who was it that suggested it? I think it was the goth boy – the tall one – the one who said he knew everybody in Edinburgh –

I said I was going to go busking around Europe and someone said 'You need a guitar' and the goth boy said he knew the shop guy who owned Scayles Music so we all trooped up there –

Bob and me and the goths and the assistant and I think by now there was a sort of tramp guy called Henry –

'Never ever smoke' – I remember him saying that, following us up the street. 'Never ever smoke – '

Fender, Gibson, acoustic, acoustic electric – everybody in the shop has an opinion about which guitar's the best and so they're bringing them all out and I'm strumming away –

Bob only knew one song.

I'm working my way through all the hits, you know – eighties stuff –

A Jesus and Mary Chain song –

And the goth kids are dancing round the shop in their strange goth twirling dance and in the end the manager brings out a beautiful crimson Gibson twelve-string and I strap it on –

(*Sings.*)

'Sun comes up another day begins and I don't even worry 'bout the state I'm in, uh huh huh.'

So Bob buys the guitar and he also buys tambourines for the goth kids, we set up a pitch on the High Street and we started busking.

Helena started handing out fivers to anybody who'd stop
and listen – fifteen tambourines and a crimson Gibson
and the Oddbins assistant's going round offering sips of
Lebanese wine, and –

Bob in the middle of it all.

Busking.

I remember he looked so happy. So happy.

JAPANESE ROPE BONDAGE

Tie me up. Tie me up
Fit your breath into mine
And I will give my secrets to you
For a night, for a night
Fit your breath into mine

Because I can do anything tonight
(Tie me up, tie me up)
Because I – can do anything tonight
Tie me up, tie me up, tie me up, tie
me up and –

It all gets a bit hazy after that.

Bob wanted some dope and the tall goth boy said he knew
a man who sold some so when he came back we all went
down the Scotsman Steps to smoke it out of the rain –

And I was telling the goth kids about seeing the Jesus and
Mary Chain play, Nicky Tams in 1983, and the kid said:

God – it must have been amazing to be alive in those
times.

There were two Icelandic students as well.

Who did the thing with the lobsters . . .

Everyone started to get hungry so we went down to the

Doric and someone says 'What's the most expensive thing on the menu?' and it turns out it's lobster.

Brilliant.

Just all of us holding up these lobsters and making them dance in a chorus line –

Twelve dancing lobsters – and the Icelandic boys singing Björk –

'It's oh so qui . . . et . . .'

One of the goth girls was a vegetarian. She got upset and I went out on the steps with her for a smoke and she said it just made her really sad to think about something living having to die, anything living, however tiny the amount of life, she said it seemed just awful that it had to die – and she was crying – and she just looked so young, so I said: 'You know we all have to die in the end, and if there wasn't death we wouldn't know that life was good,' and she said:

Yeah, duh – I realise we all have to die, lady, but how we don't need our corpses used as comedy props for a dance routine.

We went clubbing.

The tall goth boy knew a bouncer at a club somewhere down in Leith.

So we all piled into taxis. I was laughing with the wine assistant.

Taxis racing each other down Leith Walk. Henry shouting out the taxi window:

'Never ever smoke! Never ever smoke!'

And I remember thinking she just looked really happy – really really happy.

Tie me up. Tie me up
Fit your breath into mine
And I will give my secrets to you
For a night, for a night
Fit your breath into mine

Because I can do anything tonight
   (Tie me up, tie me up)
Because I – can do anything tonight
Tie me up, tie me up, tie me up, tie me
   up and –

I'm itching to be told that life does more
   than make you old
And I am itching to be told that there is
   substance in my bones
At least tonight I know that one day
   carved upon a stone
Will be the consequences of a night
   when I was not alone and –

We – can do anything tonight
We – can do anything tonight

The flier said 'Midsummer Night's Cream'. Which sounded OK so we go in.

And everyone's dressed in leather and there's a guy on all fours with a collar and chain –

And everyone's wearing masks and –

It's a fetish club – apparently.

The tall goth boy knew the DJ. Most people came for the music – apparently.

It was the Icelanders who found the Japanese rope bondage man –

Kazuo.

He was doing demonstrations in the chill-out room and the goth kids thought it would be funny put our names down.

Japanese rope bondage was invented in the twelfth century –

According to Kazuo –

As a method of interrogating prisoners. The theory of Japanese rope bondage goes like this: the tighter your body is bound, the more restricted your bodily movement and the more your mind feels like it's transcending the physical and you find your mind floating free on a sea of endorphins –

Time slows down – you lose your inhibitions – the border between you and the word seems to melt away – you feel like you're one with the universe.

And so Kazuo ties us up but then –

Something's happening in the main bar – the raffle or something –

And everybody suddenly leaves the chill-out room.

Hey!

Hey!

Wait!

Kazuo!

Kazuo!

Do you know how to do knots?

No.

Are you crying?

It's the drink. It's just the drink.

What is it?

It's fine.

It's not.

It's not OK.

What's wrong?

Maybe I'm pregnant.

Japanese rope bondage, that's how it works. You get tied up, and you lose your secrets.

Maybe.

I'm too scared to take the test but I'm late and – I don't know – I'm getting these sudden crying jags and – I feel at one with the universe and I'm finding I don't want children with leukaemia to die –

That doesn't necessarily mean you're pregnant.

No – it's different – it feels like there could be life in there.

Oh.

What if there's life in me?

Well . . .

I'd be a terrible mother.

No.

I smoke. I drink.

Maybe, but –

I'm probably pickling the poor wee thing right now.

Maybe, but –

I should be . . . eating broccoli – doing yoga –

No, I really don't think –

Look at me. What kind of mother gets drunk and smokes hash and then ends up in bondage with a petty criminal at a sex club?

Well, when you put it that way . . .

I'm scared –

Imagine something that relies on receiving love from me.

I'm not good with love.

No.

What if there's life in me – and I have to love it?

You will.

What if?

You will.

Helena?

What?

Am I the father?

What? No.

Oh.

Don't be daft.

Right.

You fucking idiot.

Yeah.

How could you be –

Yeah – how could I be.

> *Tie me up. Tie me up*
> *Press your wrists against mine*
> *Tie me up, tie me up*
> *It's time*

Because we – can do anything tonight
Because we – can do anything tonight

As soon as we're untied

Bob.

Yeah.

I think they've forgotten us.

HELP! / HELP!

4 a.m.

Eventually Kazuo heard our screaming and untied us and we left the club and went out onto the street. It was late and the two of us alone wandering in that sort of half-dark of summer, and for the first time the rain wasn't so much falling as it was hanging in the air and it felt cool on our skin after the rope burns and the club.

Bob reckoned he still had a few grand to get rid of, so we found one of those pubs where posties go – those pubs that are open at five in the morning – and Bob persuaded one guy to lend us his bag of mail, and we went down onto Leith Links and in the dark under a tree we started opening letters and slipping money into the envelopes. If there was a bill we'd put in enough to pay it – if it was a letter from a granny we'd slip in twenty more – and as we were doing it I realised that we were in the middle of the shortest night of the year.

—

Midsummer.

—

Floating on a tiny patch of night in the middle of a great sea of day, this darkness that only belonged to us.

And when the morning light came out of the haar over the Forth we took the mailbag back to the man in the pub to post and we walked up Leith Walk to the Balmoral Hotel and booked the most expensive room and as we stood and looked at the pristine bed – all white and perfect and big as a sea with the dawn making it gold-seeming, Bob lay on the bed and he looked at me and smiled and he said:

Aye, the nights are fair drawing in.

TWELVE

(*They go to bed with their clothes on. They lie next to each other for a while. They turn their backs to each other. Neither can sleep. After a time, Helena takes Bob's hand. He turns back to her. She turns her back to him so they can spoon. He holds her. They sleep.*)

(*After some time she wakes up.*)

THERE ARE ONLY INCHES BETWEEN US

It's hard enough to breathe for myself,
   darling
I cannot breathe for you as well
With my last breath I will give you my last
   kiss
But I, I cannot breathe for you as well

And there are only inches between us
But there might as well be mountains and
   trees
In this lonely distance between us
There are cities and oceans and seas

And you and me.

10.30 a.m.

Helena leaves.

THIRTEEN

(The room phone rings.)

Bob? Bob? Bob? Is that you? Bob?

So it turns out the tall goth boy who knew everybody in Edinburgh knew Tiny Tiny Tam Callaghan and this morning over breakfast in a greasy spoon off Constitution Street the tall goth boy has been telling tall stories about a woman in a bridesmaid's dress and a man with no defining features and Tiny Tiny Tam has told his father the funny story – and even though he was no psychologist, even Big Tiny Tam knows that a man with no defining features will do anything to impress a pretty girl, and so it hasn't taken much detective work for him to track Bob down to the most expensive room in the most expensive hotel in the city.

Bob?

Tam.

You. Are. Dead.

Out the fire escape – down onto Princes Street. You. Are. Dead. Down the Waverley Steps – through the crowds – out the back – there's a taxi: 'Just go anywhere, mate, anywhere.' Tam's getting a taxi as well – down Princes Street – fucking trams. I'm getting out here – the bastard's still chasing me – down to the Water of Leith – down through Stockbridge –

I can breathe later – breathing is for sissies – nobody ever died from lack of breathing –

A lot of people run for charity, this ten K may not be for Cancer Research, but Medium Bob and Big Tiny Tam are definitely running a race for life.

Because if Tam catches Bob he will kill him.

Their speeds are roughly equivalent – a slow six-mile-an-hour jog. Neither man has the necessary explosive anaerobic power to either outpace or catch up with the other. So this race has become a war of attrition.

Down through the colonies – past Canonmills –

Breathing's for sissies.

Through St Marks Park –

I can breathe later.

And in the end –

Under a bridge in Leith –

I can't go on.

Tam wins.

It seems Big Tiny Tam's Oedipal anxiety has given him a cutting edge. Looks like he just wanted it more.

Macartney, you cunt.

Tam's fist clenches and his arm begins a movement towards Bob's face, but just as it is about to connect –

Tam's heart gives out.

And whether it was the raised blood pressure caused by the grinding anxiety of his imminent filial usurpation or whether it was the sheer exertion of his run or even just time taking a very ordinary toll on an old man's body – there always has to come one breath after which there doesn't come another. And this one, now, was Tam's.

Big Tiny Tam Callaghan is dead.

And Bob looks at Tam and he thinks –

I really should go and get my Well-Man MOT.

And there are only inches between us,
But there might as well be mountains and trees
In this lonely distance between us
There are cities and oceans,
Cities and oceans,
Cities and oceans,
And seas

And you and me . . .

And these could be the best days of our lives,
So you said to me
And now we start again
Lift my head up from my knees
And look you in the eye, tell me
Could these be the best days of our lives?

And there are only inches between us
But there might as well be mountains and trees
In this lonely distance between us
There are cities and oceans
Cities and oceans,
Cities and oceans,
And seas

And you and me . . .

FOURTEEN

Helena, this is Kathy – Call me back.

Helena, this is Kathy – Call me back.

Helena, this is Kathy – Call me back.

Helena, this is Kathy, your sister by the way, and that
was my wedding you fucked up if you're sober enough
yet to remember, you bitch, and poor Brendan has just
about recovered enough to put clothes on but he's

*refusing to speak without Elmo so the least you could
do is answer your phone* – Delete.

(Text.) I need to see you. H kiss.

(Beep.) Not easy.

(Text.) I need you now.

(Beep.) Sounds sexy. Smiley face with a wink.

*(Text.) Not sexy. Face with a straight line for a mouth.
I need to talk to you.*

(Beep.) OK. Fifteen minutes.

(Text.) Where?

(Beep.) IKEA car park.

(Text.) OK.

(Beep.) Wear something red.

11.15.

The taxi drives through the morning haar that has settled
over East Lothian, and Helena can hardly see anything,
even the great blue shed is hidden like a ship in the mist,
and of course because it's Sunday morning the place is
full to brimming, and she can't see his car anywhere.

(Text.) I'm here. Where are you?

(Beep.) NW corner next to petrol station.

So eventually she gets out of the taxi into the fog and she
walks –

Where the fuck is north-west?

– round and round the car park while all around her
women loomed out of the fog – women carrying bunk
beds in foldaway boxes, women carrying bedside lights,
pregnant women with cots, and still she couldn't see
him –

(*Text*.) Am lost.

(*Beep*.) Can't miss it.

(*Text*.) I can't see you.

(*Beep*.) Need to be quick. Can't stay long.

(*Text*.) Why did you choose IKEA car park, anyway? Angry face with fist.

(*Beep*.) Convenient.

(*Text*.) Convenient???!!!

(*Beep*.) F wanted to buy candles. She's inside. Face with a hand to its mouth yawning.

Where are you?

Where are you?

Where are you?

(*Beep*.) *Welcome to Orange answerphone. You have one new message.*

Hi, it's me. Look, I'm really sorry, I waited, but then Fiona came back with the candles and I thought I might be able to persuade her to go to the canteen and get meatballs with Jack, but he gets really grisly, you know, and so I'd only said I was at the garage to get the papers and . . .

> *There are only inches between us,*
> *But there might as well be mountains and trees,*
> *In this lonely distance between us*
> *There are cities and oceans, and seas* ⌐
>
> *And you and me . . .*

And anyway, what was it you wanted to say?

(*Text*.) Bob, can I see you?

FIFTEEN

Sunday, 2.12 p.m.

Every piss artist knows that there are parts of a story that you don't tell – parts you keep back because you don't want your audience to not like your central character – specially not if the central character's you. So sometimes you keep stuff back –

There's a part of the story of the legendary night out which Helena loves –

But when Bob tells it he always misses it out.

But you need it. You need it if you're going to understand why Bob ends up on a bench on Arthur's Seat in the rain, weeping.

Rewind.

When Helena and Bob were tied together in Japanese rope bondage at Midsummer Night's Cream and Helena says to him:

You know that feeling you have where you imagine dying and as you take your last breath you think, 'What difference did I make? Is there anything I can point to on this earth and say it's better because of me?'

I know that feeling very well.

At least if you have a child you can point to the child and say – that – that life – that's better because of me.

And when Helena said that, Bob said to Helena – and she remembers it very clearly – Bob said to Helena:

Sometimes you have a kid when you're eighteen – sometimes you've bought an InterRail ticket and you're planning to go round Europe with Biggy and Jake just busking Jesus and Mary Chain songs and suddenly your girlfriend tells you she's pregnant and she asks you, 'Do you want to keep it?' and when you put it like that – well, what can you say? 'No, kill it'? So you say 'Let's get married' – and when Aidan's born it is pretty amazing holding him in your arms for about twenty minutes – but you're eighteen – you're eighteen – and anyway you kind of blame her for the whole thing and so you argue and in the end you leave each other and you probably did mean to keep in contact with Aidan but – it's hard – and maybe it's just simpler if you don't see him. And so you send his mum a cheque whenever you can and you follow his fixtures in the Lothian schools football league but – in the end – can you point to your child and say, 'This – this life is better because of me'? No. Aidan – if he's any good – that's despite me.

You have a son?

Yeah.

When Bob tells the story of Tam dying, Bob says that as Tam took his last breath he thought:

'I must make sure to go for my Well-Man MOT.'

Because that's funny. That's the feeling of the story Bob wants to convey.

But the truth is – *when Tam took his last breath Bob looked at him and thought of Aidan.*

I just needed to see him. You know.

SIXTEEN

Aidan was playing football for the Leith Academy First Eleven. Even in the fog Bob could make him out. And he called out:

Aidan.

What do you want, Dad?

I want to talk.

I'm playing football, Dad.

It's half-time.

I know.

It's my birthday.

I'm playing football.

And I didn't know what to say.

NO BALL GAMES
(*spoken word over music*)

And so I told him about where I grew up –
in the first house on the fourth floor of an
Edinburgh block of flats.

I told him there were nine floors – ten if you
count the ground like the Americans do – and
two lifts that served the floors 1, 3, 5, 7, 9 and
2, 4, 6, 8 – and around the block was a small
road that separated it from two grassy areas.

On one side the grass was used for drying
greens, but on the other side there was nothing –
just a patch of grass exactly the right size to
accommodate a game of football or rounders,
but far too big for what it actually held – a
single black pole with a double-sided wooden
sign that said:

'NO BALL GAMES'

Of course it did.

In the seventies and eighties ball games were the heroin, the crack cocaine of youth life, and vigilance was crucial. How many young lives did they ruin? How many young lives were ruined by a trip to the ice-cream van, buying some juice and using the empty can to kick around?

It's how they hook you.

Before you know it you've graduated on to using a tennis ball as a football and then you need a 'floataway', and after that nothing will do but a real pretend-leather panel-stitched ball – a 'filly' with a half-life decay that means it will lose its pristine condition and start soaking up water and doubling its weight within two weeks.

And that's when the injuries start – the aches and the sprains and the concussions.

Ball games – they ruined a generation who ignored the signs.

And this is what I told him on the playing fields in Leith –

This is what I told him.

Because I couldn't think of anything else to say.

But what I should have said was:

'We all come from the past. We all come from the past and we are all going towards the future. This is it, this is what happens – you are where you come from and you go where you go.

'This is the time travel that everyone bangs on about. It's actually happening, right here – before our eyes and underneath our feet.

'It just takes a while, that's all. It just takes a while.'

I'd better go back, they're calling me.

Yeah –

They're calling me.

Sunday, 4.15.

And now the weather with Shona. Shona –

Thanks, Drew – Well, to say it's Midsummer weekend – jings! – what a washout – particularly over central Scotland, rain with drizzle and fog all weekend – as if it was some sort of punishment – but the good news is that coming in from the east is a warmer weather-front, and so this morning's haar in Edinburgh will probably burn off by late afternoon. So if you're sitting on a bench under Salisbury Crags in the rain trying to recover from an emotional encounter with a loved one and someone texts you saying, 'Can I see you?' and you feel that tingle of excitement, and you think 'Oh no! What do I do?' – sit tight, because it looks as if the sun might actually come out – and you know what the sun does to Edinburgh, don't you? Especially in the late afternoon –

What's that, Shona?

Makes her look a peach, Drew.

Thanks, Shona.

Good news for failing men in their thirties there.

SEVENTEEN

Is this seat taken?

No.

Beautiful.

Beautiful.

Sun.

Edinburgh.

I didn't know if you'd answer my text or if you'd already gone.

Tomorrow – eleven o'clock ferry.

You know when we . . . Our first night.

Yeah.

I remember looking up and seeing my reflection in the skylight and the rain falling – pounding on the glass – hammering at the glass – and suddenly I had this feeling that I was spiralling through space towards some black hole. I felt like there was a woman – me – and she was unravelling – that as her skin was falling away a new woman, another woman, was being born – and she was raw – and her skin hurt because it wasn't used to the air – and she needed someone to hold her till she got used to it. And, well, I wanted to say thank you because – that woman – her – me – I found with her – you – and now she's OK. So anyway, I came to say thank you and goodbye.

Weekend's not over yet.

No.

Do you want to go for a walk?

Come on, we'll go for a walk.

What do you say?

Yes. I say yes.

OLD TOWN

All the people in the street
They pretend that they don't know it
They pretend that they don't know it
But it's coming anyway

And they're on their knees and praying
With their eyes towards the heavens
But God in Heaven
Cannot be found

God in Heaven
Cannot be found

So we go down
To the Old Town
You and I
Through the Old Town

And we wish
We were young again
And we wish
We were young again

And slowly fall
And slowly fall
And slowly fall into our old ways
And fall in love my love again

And slowly fall
And slowly fall
And slowly fall into our old ways
And fall in love my love again

And fall in love my love again
And fall in love my love again

Sunday night.

Bob's at the bar of the South Queensferry Brewers Fayre, body all tied up in knots, and reading Dostoevsky to cheer himself up.

Helena in her flat sitting on the lavatory with Elmo and finally takes her clear-blue test.

And it turns out there is no life in her.

EIGHTEEN

Monday, 8.30 a.m.

Bob packs his guitar and checks his passport. And waits to board the ferry to Zeebrugge.

Helena leaves her flat to go to work, to go back to the rest of her life.

Fuck shit cock piss tits.

Helena realises that her car is still parked in the Castle Terrace car park.

Helena runs.

8.46.

Helena gets to the car park.

And she puts her card in the machine –

Forty quid, fucksake, that's scandalous.

And she sees, and for the first time she understands

CHANGE IS POSSIBLE.

(*Ferry horn.*)

NINETEEN

*Let's get one thing straight. I am not going to throw
everything away and travel round Europe with you
busking Jesus and Mary Chain songs. I've booked a
really nice hotel in Bruges and two nights in Brussels and
then a flight home from Amsterdam. I'm only due a
week's holiday. OK?*

OK.

*You and I are not going to live happily ever after and this
ship is not going to sail into the sunset. Is that clear?*

Very clear.

That's what Helena said.

On the ferry to Zeebrugge.

On the Monday morning after Midsummer.

That's what she actually said – but what she really meant
to say was:

Do you need a backing singer?

Music transcription by Pete Harvey
www.cellopete.co.uk

For recordings of the songs in *Midsummer* go to
www.ponyproofrecords.com/midsummer

The Music

LOVE WILL BREAK YOUR HEART

THE SONG OF OBLIVION

HANGOVER SONG

ba ba-da ba___ ba, ba ba__ ba ba-dam,

ba ba-da bam,___ ba da-da - da dam,

FINE

ba ba-da bam,___ ba da__ da dam.___

Bob 3. If my hang-o - ver was an an-gel it would be fal - len,

If my hang-o - ver was a ship then it__ would sink,__

— If my hang-o - ver was a

feel-ing it would be last min-ute de-feat,___ and if my

D.S. al Fine

hang-o - ver was a girl it would be you.___

JAPANESE ROPE BONDAGE

G. McIntyre

♩ = 104

Tie me up, tie me up, Fit your breath in - to mine,⎯

⎯ And I will give my se-crets to you,⎯ For a night, for a night,

Fit your breath in - to mine,⎯ Be - cause

I⎯ can do a - ny - thing to - night.⎯ *(Tie me up, tie me up)*

Be - cause I⎯ can do a - ny - thing to - night.⎯

⎯ Tie me up, Tie me up, Tie me up,⎯ Tie me up.

79

Tie me up,___ And I'm itch-ing to be told___ that life does

more than make you old,___ And I am itch-ing to be told___ that there is

sub-stance in my___ bones. At least to-night I know that one day

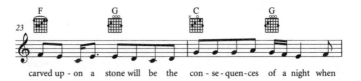

carved up-on a stone will be the con-se-quen-ces of a night when

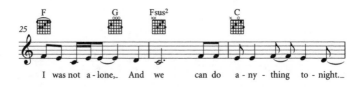

I was not a-lone,___ And we can do a-ny-thing to-night.___

___ We can do a-ny-thing to-night.___

Tie me up, Tie me up,

Press your wrists a-gainst mine.

Tie me up, Tie me up, Fit your breath a-round mine.

Be - cause we___ can do a - ny - thing to-night.__

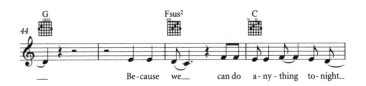

___ Be - cause we___ can do a - ny - thing to-night.__

___ As soon as we're un - tied.___

THERE ARE ONLY INCHES BETWEEN US

look you in___ the eye,___ tell me: Could these be the best_

___ days of our lives?_

And there are on-ly inch-es be-tween us, But there

might as well be moun-tains and trees.___ In this

lone-ly dis-tance be-tween us, There are ci-ties and o - ceans,

ci - ties and o - - ceans, ci - ties and o - - ceans and

seas.___ And you and me.

NO BALL GAMES

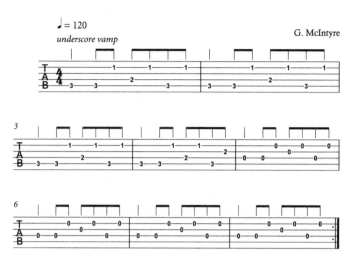

OLD TOWN

♩ = 108   G. McIntyre

All the peo-ple in the street,—

They pre-tend that they don't know it,

They pre-tend that they don't know it,

But it's co-ming a-ny-way.—

And they're on their knees and pray-ing,

With their eyes to-wards the hea-vens,   But God in Hea-